Poems A Journey of Ages

Robert Hicks

ISBN:0615597319
ISBN-13:
978-0615597317

≈

DEDICATION

This book is dedicated to my parents who are always there to support me. To my best friend Julia and my friend Kayla who helped inspire me to finish this book. Lastly to life for without this book wouldn't have been written.

CONTENTS

ACKNOWLEDGMENTS

One Less Reason, Machinae Supremacy, Lifehouse, and Delain for their music has helped inspire me in my poetry.

1 ROMANCE

A Day for Lovers

The sky was beautiful today the warm of the sun as warm as the hair on
her cheek.

Clouds hover overheard creating images of beauty and telling the tales
of the world
Looking into those green eyes looking brighter then the grass in which
they lay.
Smiles can't be oppressed love to great to give in.
The touch of her skin melts me like butter.
"When you are next to me I am never weak." she whispers."
"When you are next to me you are my world." she replies.
Standing up tickling each other as they laugh and they play.
Today is a joyous day celebrating where their relationship began.
Beauty so wonderful like the wings of butterfly do flutter.
Lips join one has louder than any words can speak.
Lifting back her hair as it does curl.
The colors of their clothes showing they support each other without
delay.
Emotion so grand set out on display.
On her shirt she places with the words of love you written on the pin

After All

Times were good
You were my friend
Through the toughest of times we stood hand and hand
Laughter filled the sea of caring

After all we been through why do you have to be this way?
Of kin we danced through the enemy
Now we are the ones on the opposite sides
Covered now in a blanket of sin
Things could have worked we could have remained
After all we been through why do you have to be this way?
Fear was not an option only a state of mind
Voices now linger in a time now forgotten
Memories flicker like a camera flash
Stood together now standing tall alone
After all we been through why do you have to be this way?
Cool love turned into burning hatred
Smiles now cracked being stuck by the hammer
Hearts now twisted in a vine of lies
Mind shut down in shock and awe
After all we been through why do you have to be this way?
Your gift is now my curse
Life will not be the same
Corruption now fills the sea of caring
Blood on both our hands, but mine are not as stained
After all we been through why do you have to be this way?
Betrayed by a beast once called a friend
I am the animal now hunted
Chew out my throat so that I may breathe tonight
Bitter sweet is the ending
After all we been through why do you have to be this way?

Anything

You came into my life beauty flowing so bright. That wonderful voice calling my name takes away all of my pain. Your presence encompasses me reminds me what my existence is supposed to be. I go to bed every night knowing that everything is going to be alright.

You are the essence of me you are what makes me breathe. We have become so apart I would do anything to help you.

When you need a shoulder to lean on, a friend to talk to, or a helping hand when you fall I will be there for you. I will do

2

anything to make you safe. I will protect you from the evils of this place. When you break down and cry I will be there to help you to fly. I will help to dry all tears, I will be there to fight away all your fears, and I will always be there until the end of years.

If you ever need me call I will come running and save you from troubles, because someone like you shouldn't have to go all this shit and I will help to shovel it away. Just remember I am just a call away day or night I am here for you to help to make you feel alright.

You are the essence of me you are what makes me breathe. We have become so apart I would do anything to help you.

Beauty Within Sorrow

Lying on the couch crawled up in a blanket, staring at the blankness in the wall, and tears streaming down my face like a waterfall. Feeling all hope lost my very being was sucked into an unknown vacuum, in which I free fall forever-in despair.

Being alone trying to find myself in the endless dark. Tripping over many sharp objects along the way, bringing pain-making torture look like fun. Finally falling and having a knife fly straight through my heart. Bleeding by torment of this world, tasting the fear my heart, and the blood that flows from the deep opened wounds that continue to flow like lava down a volcano.

Feeling like my existence is vanished I fall back into a blackened corner. In there I swim in the vast lake of tears, choking on the tears as they rush inside of me. Closing my eyes as I fall away to place inside myself. Looking beneath it all, I see the beauty I possess. Questions racing through my head like a speeding bullet. Are they blind, can they not feel or see what I possess inside of me? Emotionally, physically, and mentally beaten down by the people of this world.

Why live at all when you just walk around like a dead and broken soul slumbering around so weak you can barely stand. Being hated by many people rage building up inside, and it will only go off like a stick of dynamite sooner or later and blow up everything around it. Then there is the sadness that flows through out of me like raging rivers that flood my soul, in which I drown and die.

Drowning deep inside being pushed under by raging waters, taking one last gasp for air and then I open my eyes. A brilliant light flashing upon my eyes blinding me, and then I close them again. Upon opening them again, I see the light is the radiant aura of beauty that flows from one of the most gorgeous angels ever. Her smile lighting up the day, brighter then the sun's rays could ever do. I look through her eyes deep down inside and see inner beauty more beautiful and perfect then Eden itself.

Inside her embrace brings warmth that protects me from all the coldness that the world has to offer. Inside her embrace our love intertwines in a bright flash of light sending a sonic boom that drives away all the darkness that eclipsed our hearts. Planting seeds of love, hope, and happiness where the darkness once stood. Every moment we spend together is pure bliss and is so magical.

Dazzling array of love so sparkling and perfect makes the most perfect diamond seem flawed. I feel her in my heart wherever I go it seems as if she is the one that keeps my heart beating. The times spent away it feels like a part of me has been lost, but as soon as I see that sparkling aura of love it is quickly found again. I wish I would have known angels like her was on this Earth all along, then I would I have known I was in Heaven the whole time.

Doorway to a soul

Look into my eyes tell me what you see, there is another world inside of me locked away so deep.

Very little things make me happy, and sadness is what my heart
seems to keep.
Every night I lie down and cry, wondering if I should live or die.
Feeling the caress of loneliness touch me, wanting to have
someone to rescue me and set me free.
To be able to grab a hold of someone's hand to be where it would
seem like time wasn't moving and the sound of laughter would be
so soothing.
To be with another in a relaxing walk, or just sit for hours and just
talk.
Be lost in moments without a care just as long as someone was
there.
Maybe I am just dreaming, but I know someday it will come where
I won't be so sad and have something good instead of bad.

Dragon Kisses

Eyes lost in a world of confusion head hammered like a contusion
Wars waged internal within fangs and sharp claws at the ready dripping
with sin
Boots worn from the miles of travel breaths becoming to unravel

I will fight to the end with my strength your honor I will defend
Through an army of undead with each and every blow your love I will
spread
Love just isn't what it used to be withered like snow on a tree

Oh I just want to know what it feels like to kiss a dragon!
Spread your wings and fly with me so many scenic sites left unseen!

Instead of embracing me a loser you declared thee
Nostrils filled smoke fire breathed so you could not choke
Sword drops to the ground a barely beating heart the only sound

Oh I just want to know what it feels like to kiss a dragon!
Spread your wings and fly with me so many scenic sites left unseen!

Why can't you believe that I love you is really that hard to be true
I know I made mistakes love why can't you forgive me dove

I traveled the labyrinth maze now standing in front you I am the haze

The treasure I unearthed please just listen to our rebirth
I am not your prince nor are you my princess
Two peasants been through a lifetime of sorrow a locket of faith I have
borrowed

I just want to know what feels like to kiss a dragon!
Spread your wings and fly with me so many scenic sites left unseen!

This should be our fate instead you're filled with so hate
I fought for you would die for you and you tell me just to shoo
Darling can't you see that my heart longs for thee

On the other side of sight all along I was on the wrong side of the fight
Days begin to simmer nights are getting dimmer
To the beast I turn my skin begins to burn

I just want to know what it feels like to kiss a dragon!

Spread your wings and fly with me so many scenic sites left unseen!

Dreams are made of

The world is wide and blue
Often times not hitting the cue
Today is the day that I rue
Not sure what is true
Emotions spread out flew
A stone I threw
Her face the only one that I knew

Oh Oh when it all comes crashing down
And I feel like giving in
She said that is what dreams are made of

This path I have walked
These things that I have talked
On this board things that have chalked
My future seems to be blocked
The key to my heart the only one ever locked
My whole life I have been mocked

It seems that my time has been clocked

Oh Oh when it all comes crashing down
And I feel like giving in
She said that is what dreams are made of

I am always the living the joke
Teased and constantly poke
The drugs I refused to smoke
My friends' wonder who is this bloke
Fallen like the leaves of an oak
Tear stained eyes they do soak
Breathless air I do choke

Oh Oh when it all comes crashing down
And I feel like giving in
She said that is what dreams are made of

She said don't be afraid to be yourself
All these hollow feeling you need shelf
Live like a fantasy like you're the only Elf

Oh Oh when it all comes crashing down
And I feel like giving in
She said that is what dreams are made of

She let your colors shine brighter than any sun
Dance around and have some fun
After all life is loaded gun

Oh Oh when it all comes crashing down
And I feel like giving in

She said that is what dreams are made of.

Everything So Beautiful

I take a walk outside today, feeling the cool breeze blow my way. The birds are singing so beautiful, it is such a heavenly tune and if I sing with them it makes me wonder away. Looking down I see a flower sway. It looks so beautiful and it smells so pure, I get lost in its lure. I feel the sun's rays the warmth like a bathing cure. I close my eyes and it strips me of all my senses and all the pain I endured. I know the reason for such a beautiful day is because of you. I feel you in my heart even though we are so far apart. It makes me happy, makes me whole, and it makes me wonder:

Why is everything so beautiful have to be so far away, looking across the skies hoping they will bring me into your arms to stay. Seeing you day by day knowing everything good is coming my way. You are so beautiful inside to out. More beautiful and perfect then any angel someone could dream about. Feeling the love from you it's so warm and pure, makes my heart skip a beat as our together our love meets. Every word you speak means so much to me. My heart sees that every word you speak you mean. My heart is beating, my lungs are breathing, and my mind is thinking and it's all because of you.

I love you more each and every day knowing you are there makes me feel OK and keeps the sadness and the pain away.
Why is everything so beautiful had to be so far away, looking across the skies hoping they will bring me into your arms to stay.

Headlights To Heaven

Ten years down the road, since that awful tragedy.
I still see the images in my head of that night.
How can I forget it, the night that destroyed my life?
We were out for a midnight drive to meet with some friends.
Hearing that dreaded screeching noise, and seeing something serve back in forth in the distance.
You held on to me to tight, scared to death.
Then I see lights heading our way, slamming away the one I loved.

These headlights were your ticket to heaven, but you were so young, why did it have to be this way? I miss you.

Waking as if from a nightmare, I saw you next to me.
I yell out your name, shake you, but you were motionless.
Tears streaming down my face, how could this have happened?
Hoping everything will be all right, my entire body filled with fright.
Hearing someone yell, seeing the rescue team arrive.

These headlights were your ticket to heaven, but you were so young, why did it have to be this way? I miss you.

Tuesday, February 26, the day my life was left in shambles, taking away all that I loved.
Everyone thinks drunk driving is a game, its fun to play.
Let's see you on the other side, will you still enjoy then, and I don't think you will.
When someone gets hurt the games stop, and reality sinks in.
I always keep wondering if we didn't go that night, will everything still be the same.

I Can Not Recall

I can't recall the last time we have spoken
I can't recall the smell of your perfume
I can't recall the color of your eyes
I can't recall the taste of your lips
I can't recall the last time I seen you sway those hips
I can't recall the last time I smiled
I can't recall the last time I danced
I can't recall the last time I sang
I can't recall what your voice sounds like
I can't recall your name
I can't recall when things will ever be the same
I can't recall the last time we played a game
I can't recall the last time emotions were sacrificed
I can't recall the love of your heart
I can't recall your hair
I can't recall the times we spent together

However I can recall how much I miss you.

I Would Just For You

Words have spoken
But did you hear
I will be right beside you my only dear
Let us hold hands there is nothing to fear
Wipes of those cheeks no need to shed a tear
In the darkness you are my flare
In deaths eyes I would glare

I would walk across the fiery coals for you
I would weather the storm just for you
I would bleed myself dry just for you

Whisper gently to me
Open my eyes so that I can see
Touch me so that I can feel
Be my doctor help me to heal
You have the key to open my heart
You are the waves from not washing us apart
You are the keeper of my soul
The one to make this shattered mirror whole
You love me without being told
In your arms I want to forever hold

I would sail across the ocean just for you
I would grow wings and fly just for you
I would always tell the truth just for you

My dearest Michelle
You be the one keeping from being dragged to Hell
You are the scars from every time I feel
The only one whose secrets I would tell
You make me feel better when I was not well

I would love you forever just for you
I would always be your angel just for you
I would always be the beacon of hope in the blindest of night just for you

I would do this all just for you my dear.

If I Leave

Out caste by everyone, my feelings blasted, not even the greatest of happiness lasted. Oh, tell me why, can't anything ever go so right, my body is shattered with fright, and my mind is shut down so tight. Am I being tested by some sick game, you give me everything I have ever wanted, and then took it back as if it never came. I don't think anyone even gives a care, praying to someone my soul to claim; maybe death will give me that much-needed glare. Oh, tell me if I leave this place, to fade away without a trace, and finally release me from torment and the pain, would you miss me. I know you most likely won't, always having that sick smile on your face, knowing this hatred was killing me, spilling distraught emotions throughout me. I know you don't care; you are never there, anyway, always sitting alone day after day. My lungs now seemed filled with clay, so I lay my final rest, now I will leave you to see if you can pass the test, but before I go I write one last final farewell, Oh, tell me if I leave this place, to fade away without a trace, and finally release me from torment and the pain, would you miss me.

If You Could Only Feel

Deep within the abyss the lava rumbles

Temperatures cold as ice create images hanging from the ceiling
Indents in the ground marking my arrival
Breaths in the air marking my departure
If you could only feel my sadness
Roaring is the hurricane of the soul into the eyes of liars
Decent into the cave of madness has begun
Scaling the mountain of faith has been a failure
The stench lingers on flaring in the nostrils
If you could only feel my sadness

Sad happy is the way I am
Tears of ice covered fire rain down onto the village of hope
Things could be easy, but then what would we learn
Time has vanished replaced by a void
If you could only feel my sadness
Beating is the heart that has been tarnished
Lungs filled with love even after the torture
Forgiveness in the hands of the fallen
Reaching out for you to do the same
If you could only feel my sadness
What did I do wrong to be treated this way?
Why do you hate me so?
Why must I be beaten on display for misunderstanding?
Why can't you see how beautiful I am?

If you could only feel my sadness.

IOU My Heart

Oh radio my radio play me my favorite tune

Sing me a lullaby filled with cheer
Show me your brilliant smile
Cover my ears from the things I do not need to hear
Open my eyes to world of make believe
Help me sing out my worries
Help me dance out my tears
Flow through me like a surge of energy
Tell me about friendship
Tell me about heartache
Listen to my words even though they mean nothing
In this moment the sun will always shine
Protect me from the clouds that would do me harm
The tales you tell are but a perfect memory
With much love from me to you
Tonight dear radio I owe you my heart.

Journey

Empty hollow eyes close slowly

Filled with thoughts of emotion
Pouring throughout the skies
Casting shades of many colors

A breeze passes by a man
Standing alone in a field
Expanding many miles
Leading to paths far and wide

Faces see smiles appear either of acceptance or displace
Confusion swims throughout the rivers
Running downstream to lakes
Lakes surrounding in a cool embrace

Animals scurry on the land
Lost to their own tasks
Grass sways gently in the wind
Telling stories of old and new

"So what do you think?" calls the man
Hearings of words go unnoticed
"Hey over here" the man calls again
Looks of curiosity loom forth

"Will you join me?" asks the man
Walking closer the shadow looms near
"Hello there." Replies the woman
A nod followed by a smile follows

"What do you say we explore this land?" asks the man
A hand is extended outward
"We shall see." Replies the woman
Always hanging the hand waits.

Love Of The Phoenix

Crash burned oh my has my world turned
Ashes to ashes dust to dust my soul is beginning to rust
Hope still lingers on the phoenix has arisen from the ashes of
memories
Spread across the divide new life it will provide
I shall never give up someday its wings will fly
One day to finally show me the true way
Sitting and waiting forever to be back the way it was again.

If you nurture the rays of light happiness will never fade
A blade of grass grows everyday eventually to make a field of
memories
Parts of the field will burn with time
If you nurture the rays flowers shall bloom from the destruction
Sands tick down each and every hour
Only to fill up on the other end
What will save us from sinking beneath the sand
The love of the phoenix and the hands of whom we can depend.

Moonlit Night

An owl flies by the window telling me things will be all right
To the outside I then run the racing of my heart has begun
Standing outside patiently waiting for her to show
Feeling the warmth of the moon on a cool winter night
The sensation of the glow filling me with such delight
Snow canvases around the courtyard creating a brilliant circle
Rabbits scurry about in the bushes light rustling to be heard
Beginning to wonder I start to think where is she my heart starts to
sink
Staring at the moon the owl flies by again telling me it will all right
A feather glides down onto my hand confidence I regain
Shimmering smile crosses my face across the courtyard footsteps
trace

Shining bright with the moon she walks towards me
Coming closer she grabs me by the waist
Putting the feather into her hair she smiles greatly with warmth of
care
There is no better feeling than being close to the one you love
It is even better waltzing under a cool moonlit night.

My Heart Belongs To You

My feelings are fluid
Yesterday my heart beats

Happiness begins to rise
Enough of this pointless dream
Allowing for reality to take its place
Reaching out for the touch of love
Traveling the roads of my imagination

Before now it was self emptiness
Elongated is a spindle of fate
Lifting up the stones of doubt
Only if you speak those three words
Not with holding the sacred grove
Given the chance to live again
Search is over I have found you

Tell me you will have me
Occasionally surprise me

Yearning is beneath me
On this day I stand tall once more
Understand the dream is over.

Our Own Fantasy

With this ring I thee wed
Yes you have said
Together we will be always
Even death can't separate us
I love you with all of my heart
With all of my soul
Let's forget about the past because baby our future is bright
Now stand up and let us dance together

Our minds are filled with thoughts
Before we know it
We are lost in our own fantasy

Life is such bitter shame
When is the baggage going to be claim?
I am just who I am
At the bottom of the sea the only clam
I love you till the bitter end
With my life I will defend
Now open your voice and sing with me

Our minds are filled with thoughts
Before we know it
We are lost in our own fantasy

These halls I walk all I by myself
In these woods I am the only Elf
No one will understand
Why I am stranded here on this land
Emotions run wild in this book
Trying to find myself through every nook
Now let us all bring it together

Our minds are filled with thoughts
Before we know it
We are lost in our own fantasy

I am truly special
The abomination of uncertainty
The creature hunting in the night
The voice without a whisper
Now everyone let us hear your voice

Our minds are filled with thoughts
Before we know it
We are lost in our own fantasy

Our minds are filled with thoughts
Before we know it
We are lost in our own fantasy

Our minds are filled with thoughts
Before we know it
We are lost in our own fantasy

In our own fantasy we can be whatever we want to be.

Our Worlds
There are worlds inside our hearts
Where hopes looms and love conquers all
Guardians of our world we unite
Strong willed and brave not afraid
Not many people see our world
For they do not understand the beauty
That exists inside us all so inside their hearts they fall
Layers to the world to explore always changing
Joy, fun, and childhood laughter fill the streets
Houses made of memories
People made of thoughts
Objects made of ideas
Storms may caress on our doubt but prevail we will
These are our worlds so special so true

How many people have seen your world?

Passing Of Lives

Shimmering light from the sun and the moon
Dancing over all things playing images on a screen
Down below silent eyes stare up to watch the plays
Up above lost eyes stare down to watch the plays

Always looking at the same thing but the eyes never meet

Silent screams of pain drift down touching the ground
Hopeful whispers float towards the skies
Mixture of sound always passing with the same message
Never interloping they go unnoticed to never reach its destination
Blown away with the winds to be lost with time

Knowing how to descend down from the perch
Knowing how to ascend up to the perch
Separate ladders they do take to never see
Passing by another, but never knowing
To descend from the perch, and then to ascend to it

Places to be always traded in the waltz of time
One day the ladders will bump together
For the first time they will finally see
That they should have looked up, instead of always staring down
Separate ways will they continue to go, or will they choose the
same path only time will show.

Poem

Out of respect afraid to say the thoughts swarming in the mind
can't speak them aloud
Light appearing from endless time feelings of warm and kind
whisperings of sound
Steady shaking hands create a world of magical beauty where
blank walls once stood
Doubt plagues within the mind, but rest assure what has been
created is very good.

Silence covers the face with all the thoughts in a race
Always lost to the world around due to the deafening hums of the
place
Being lost inside the maze feels like wisdom has escaped always

being teased
Great wisdom grows from silence leaving seeds of creativity all around leaving those who see the flowers bloom pleased.

In the shade this one hides always between here and the divide
Afraid to come out of the shelter and see what the world can provide
With time the shade will become thinner, and underneath the eyes will see a winner
Remarkable aspects this one does posses, but to close to the shadow to see it by oneself always sitting alone thinking only of dinner.

If the eyes only looked up they would see across the yard another tree
Someone else sits down inside the shade wishing for someone to come and be
Deep inside both are afraid to accept something different beyond their own tree
Silent whispers echo inside tormenting with doubts, and with glee.

Seasonal Angel

I made a snow angel of you to tell of your heart
To show off your kindness
To show what you mean to me
To show that your love warms my coldest days
To show that even through the toughest of times you are there
To show how fun you can be
To show how beautiful you are
To show the blessing of life
To show that you are my angel no matter what

I made a sand angel of you to tell of your mind

To show how smart you are
To show how much wisdom you possess
To show off the advice you have given
To show how a little grain can make a difference
To show how your love warms my heart
To show that you are always a step ahead
To show your intellectual beauty as well
To show off childhood memories
To show off how lovely your smile can be

You are my seasonal angel your wings always lift my spirit high.

Someone Special

Every night I lay down and cried, closing my eyes I prayed for an
angel I prayed for a special someone, a someone to be with me
someone to like me for me and nothing else. Day after day my
hopes shattered, my feelings battered tears running down my face,
thick as blood, and then they vanish without a trace. Depression
consuming me, happiness longing to be free, blinking away the
tears that are wanting to get out of me.

Opening up my eyes I see the most beautiful girl. Feeling like my
prayers have been answered, talking to you seemed like heaven.
Looking through my eyes seeing perfection, drying up all of my
internal cries. Hearing your voice, making me drift away. Every
moment with you is pure joy, even the places I wish I couldn't stay
seem so great. For the first time in awhile I smile, I'm happy. It
seems as though fate brought you into my embrace, to make me
forget all of the horrors of this place.
I love you with all my heart; I hope we never grow apart.

Thinking about you all the time, lost in the thoughts of the beauty
of you. When you're with me I'm no longer sad, but glad to have
met someone as special as you. My love for you runs so pure and
true, hoping that one day I can be with you to look into the face of

beauty, hold you into my arms, and be with you forever, because you're the one in which my heart desires.

Squeeze You

The invasion has begun
With open arms I accept
The troops of hate
Marching on towards the lake
Bitterness the only beating sun
Always was a failure even now never adept
Time to assimilate
Should of though before I acted didn't realize what is at stake

I miss you
I love you
Next time I see you
I just want to squeeze you

I forgot how this all began
Just want to be in yours again
The troops of regret
Marching down the stream of denial
So hot I need a fan
Feet blistering walking the sand
Worry filled wounds with fret
Life is always trial

After a while
I miss you
I love you
Next time I see you
I just want to squeeze you

All I know is you are my shining knight on the steed
Candied eyes open to sweet misery
The Colonel of happiness did declare
It's not your fault my child
Open your heart and you will be free
Candied lips speak the truth of rivalry
The Colonel he said light up your soul like a flare
Sometimes love is just spicy and mild

These words ring true
I miss you
I love you
Next time I see you
I just want squeeze you

I just want to see your pretty face
Disappear with you with a trace
Forget all this nonsense the disgrace
Play the Wii at my place
I can be leather and you can be the lace

Shout it at the top of my lungs
I miss you
I love you
Next time I see you
I just want to squeeze you

I just want to squeeze you

Sweet Dreams

We were both young and hopelessly in love.
Holding you in my arms, seeing the glitter in your eyes.
Feeling your heart as it beats against my chest.
Feeling the warmth from your body, as we lay cheek to cheek.
Tonight was the greatest night, I said to you.
Seeing your lips let out that brilliant smile, kissing them softly.
Then I say to you, sweet dreams I love you.

Fast-forward five years along we had a loving family.
Bringing the greatest of joys to each other, throughout the years.

Watching our kids grow up to be fine, memories in my heart
forever entwined.
I still remember the first time we met, engraved in my heart for
eternity.
Now each and every waking moment, is just like heaven with you.
Sure we have had our ups and downs, but at least we learned to
help each other out.
Every night I still say to you, sweet dreams I love you.

Time as taken its toll; we are now aged in our years.
However I am sick, lying on my deathbed.
I see the sadness in your eyes, all of those internal cries.
I don't know how many more breaths I can take.
I hold your hand and say to you, sweet dreams I love you.

Sweet Melody

I hear a heavenly tune calling from somewhere. Wishing I could go
there. Knowing it to be some place safe some place warm.
Listening to the song makes me fly across the sky telling me things
can never go wrong.

The sound of it so sweet and soothing makes my feet lift up off the
ground. My life feeling like a feather the sound of the melody
drowning out all the bad weather.

Your love is like a sweet melody every sound you make, my
presence you take. Getting lost in a trance as my heart begins to
dance; it screams you are the one lost so long ago in my dreams.

The sound of the melody so beautiful brings tears my eyes, as my
soul cries. Tears of bliss rather than sorrow as I forever stay in a
moment like this. Makes me know tomorrow will be OK as the
melody embraces me giving me a feeling of security.

The melody sounds so far away but I feel it next to me
encompassing me taking me away to a forgotten place.
Your love is like a sweet melody every sound you make, my
presence you take. Getting lost in a trance as my heart begins to
dance; it screams you are the one lost so long ago in my dreams.

Take Me Away

Living alone lost in a void of confusion, my existence-shattered
pieces falling away from me. Broken down deep inside of me I
hear a voice that takes me to a place I rather be. Beauty pouring
down like rain, the look on your face takes away all the pain, your
presence keeps me from going insane.
I love you with all my heart and soul you have fixed the shattered
pieces and made me whole.

Take me away to a special place where dreams come true, but my
dreams will come true as long as I'm with you.
Every breath you take keeps my life awake; the smile upon your
face takes me away to a special place. I could stay forever in a
moment like this, your presence watching over me, sets my soul
free. When you are around my heartbeats, my life reaches amazing
feats.

I love you with all my heart and soul you have fixed the shattered
pieces and made me whole. Take me away to a special place where
dreams come true, but my dreams will come true as long as I'm
with you.

Who Is There

Falling down on my knees pains stinging like a swarm of bees. Staring down the darkened hole, my heart choking on a piece of coal it's blackened like night suffocating taking away all my might. Fading away because in this place I can't stay about to leave it all before I finally stumble and fall, but then I remember that very special call. Closing my eyes letting all my defenses fall remembering what I heard and saw. Feeling your love making my pain fly away like a dove.

Who is there to help me up when I stumble and I fall who is there to make me forget it all. It is you only you. It is your beauty that lights up the hole it is that radiance that makes me feel whole. My spirit soars, all the sadness flies out an open door no longer feeling the rain pour.
One word your heart speaks makes me hear the most beautiful sound as my feet lift off of the ground. Every time I see you I free fall deeper into your love falling from the heavens above. I pray that when I reach the bottom it will be in your arms to stay. When you are away a part of me missing and I don't feel whole no more. I miss you so much longing to feel that sweet touch.

Even though you are not here you still take away all my fear and every last droplet of tear because
Who is there to help me up when I stumble and I fall who is there to make me forget it all. It is you only you. It is your beauty that lights up the hole it is that radiance that makes me feel whole. My spirit soars, all the sadness flies out an open door no longer feeling the rain pour.

2 NATURE

Answer To The Tornado

It's getting hot
It's getting heavy
It's getting rainy
It's getting windy

Tell me can you control the wind
When the heavens start to spin

Run when you hear the roar
When no longer see the birds soar
Shelter in your hands no need to a tour
Hands over heads down onto the floor
Started as one now up to four
Storms over my head flirting with allure

Tell me can you control the wind
When the heavens start to spin

Buildings are destroyed
Lives are lost
Too much to bear to much the cost
Deadly are these winds
When they from a funnel
Eyes become a tunnel
As the fear sets in

Tell me can you control the wind
When the heavens start to spin

Then it all comes bearing down
A train the only sound
The house shakes violently
Pictures fall to the ground
The dog to scared to bark
Everything has gone dark
We are the target it has its mark

Tell me can you control the wind
When the heavens start to spin

Tell me can you tell me
I need to know the answer.

Nature's Orchestra

A bird sits chirping a merry song
And soon other animals chime in along
A chorus of beautiful music so soothing
Array of colors cascading waves so rooting
Away goes the trouble of the world so dim
Awaiting is the happiness worn so slim

A bird sits as the conductor of harmony
Animals become the orchestra of calm
And soon peace blows over the land in testimony
Awarding those who listen to the melody and clap with palm
Awaiting of the cheers the animals wait the conductor sits on the
plank
All of them working making the world a better place, I would like
to thank.

The Sun

Bright

Yellow
A star like no other
Warm
Comforting
Ray of dreams
Radiant hope
Always there even through the dark
Look up to you when things don't seem good.

Wind

Cool
Warm
Strong
Weak
Harmless
Destructive
Peaceful
Chaotic
North
South
East
West
Fly a kite
Feel the breeze
Sail Away
Stay Ashore
Calm

Winter

Dandruff is falling upon the Earth again
Time for everything rest
So they revitalize beauty upon this Earth again
White flakes flowing so slowly so soothing
So cold outside but still warmer then most things
Even in the harshness beautiful life still looms
Can you see beyond the veil of white?
To notice the wonderful things that exists?

3 OTHER

Been Awhile

It has been awhile since I have written
Not much to say not much happening
Just been here all along watching and sitting
A lot has gone on but nothing all at once
Hello to all and hello to none
Things go good here happiness without fear
Will write more soon with much to say
Without saying much at all.

Itchy

Itching to write but not sure what to write
Mind goes blank then freezes
So many ideas swimming around my head
At the tip of the tongue ready to bite
Hands at the ready to began air blows past in the breezes
All things swimming in the head now vanishes with nothing to be said.

The Poet And The Pen

One is mighty the other wise
Both stained with ink
Words come to life with motion
Tip of beauty rests in the hand
Black becomes the new dawn
As horizons are expanded
Time has no meaning to the length
Emotional is the emotionless object
Fingers meet a storybook shaft of tales
Memories forged in the fires of letters
Creator or martyr only the one who speaks knows
Round is the base in which destiny has no name
Thoughts are born in a vortex of color
You cannot use one without using the other
Speech has no comprehension in this voice
Traveling on a journey yet to be defined
Eyes cannot see what only the beholder already knows
So who is doing the talking is it the poet or the pen?

The Will

The will that keeps the clock ticking has almost burnt its gears

The will for happiness is being eaten by madness

The will for hope is nothing but a faded dream

The will for being wanted leaves me an outcast

The will for helping leaves me to wonder why I am the bad guy in the end

The will to be there always leaves me to sold on the black market

The will to be smarter just leaves me in a maze of confusion

The will to be perfect leaves me in doubt

The will to bring laughter helps me to forget pain
The will to be calm leaves me a furious beast

The will to stop tears just lets someone else open the valve further

The will to be alone always brings unwanted company

The will to smile is always back slapped to a frown

The will to be lost in my own little world helps me to escape troubled times

The will for death keeps me alive

The will reminds me of how my life is never supposed to worth anything.

Zazbun

This is the story of Zazbun

Who only weighed a ton
Despite his size he loved to have fun
Practical jokes he used as his gun
Because of this the friends he had was one

More often than not he would get into trouble
With his jokes burying himself underneath the rubble
Five o clock shadows usually cast not speaking of his stubble

Often imitated people try to be his double

One day his jokes went too far he splashed into the lake creating quite a puddle
The townspeople talked beginning to huddle

They told Zazbun if he didn't stop they would him from the city
Zazbun stuck out his tongue shouting man this is shitty
The townspeople smirked man a pity

The next Zazbun played a trick on the mayor putting his car on the roof
Everyone knew it was him they didn't need the proof

The townspeople did declare you banned
Stretching out his wings he did spanned

With a tear on his cheek he set to find a new home
The townspeople rejoiced with his departure reclaiming their home.

4 WORDS
THIS CHAPTER IS UNIQUE SPINS ON BAD WORDS TO HELP THINK OF THEM IN MORE POSITIVE LIGHT.

Nice person
Interesting ideas
Great talent
Gifted
Enlisted to help others
Real American civilian.

Beauty
Internal triumph
Trusted friend
Caring just don't know how to express
Helping out the homeless.

A friend in need
Self creative
Slow, but quickly with the mind
Honest with their words
Open hear-ted
Leaving no stone unturned
Elegant.

Caring
Understanding
Never giving up

True to themselves.

Great personality
Awesome individual
Young at heart forever.
Friendly
Unit of love
Child of dreams
Kip up of hope
Enveloped with a smile
Rescuer of the innocent.

Having a heart of gold
Allowed for dreams to shine
Tracker of lies
Entertainers we love
Respected people of society.

Lover of the best kind
Enough of a friend to last lifetimes
Strong willed
Bringer of faith
In eyes of beauty
Allowed of choices
Next best friendship.

Wonderful person
Enlightened joy
Intellectual
Real American hero
Driven by passion.

Lover
Interesting
Alive with desire
Reality story tellers.

A home is like a lillypad ever flowing but always stationary
Hopping along the way the frogs come and go
Open waters surrounded by purity
Most may see even in the toughest moments what a home may be
Encased inside the walls for lifers every moment we experience.

You are
A lifeless bump on the log
Mindless in self doubt
Allowing nothing into your heart
Zeroing in on a target of worthlessness
Interloping in the fields of sorrow
Never allowing a smile
Great loneliness in a sea of pity

But you can be
A log that isn't a bump but lively
Mindful your excellent quality
Allow for things into your heart if for the right reasons
Zero in on the target of usefulness
Interlope in the fields of happiness
Never allow a frown
Great happiness in a sea of pride.

Art is beautiful no matter where it comes from
Radiant and wonderful truly a gift to behold
Traditional or not everyone is beautiful

Insight gives us reason to create
Silent whispers bloom into new life

Blessed is every creation brought onto this Earth
Erased and used but ever triumphant
A smile vibrant like a rainbow
Untie the knots of love and let it flow through you
Thanks are not enough for the gifts we get to see
Infamous are the prints left by our fingers
Fruitful are the blessing in which we receive
Understand this is your dream let it come alive
Live life to the fullest and remember this because like art you are
beautiful.

Art is love no matter where it comes from
Remembrance or new stories to tell
Trades and requests are decided
In a line they are created
Sketched or written

Tongues are the not thing to speaks words
Inside these wall magic is created
Creations from everyone filled with joy

State what is one your soul
Tally the totals of your ideas
Across oceans stories to tell
Together we are one
Enjoyment looking at the pieces
Mental or physical things do happen
Eclipsed is the shadow hovering over the pen
No idea shall escape
Truths and lies are told.

Born
Exceptional
And
Understanding
Thoughts of
Yourself.

Broken is only the tip of a mountain of emotion
Recovered from a waste less sea of doubt
Order of society given way to chaos of savages
Ketchup smeared across the chest of humanity
Each his own in this epic struggle
News and highlights from a life lost along the road.

You are my:
Befriending
Understanding
Dependable
Diligent
Youthful.

Bouncing bundle of joy
Underneath the fur a heart of gold
Never sad always moving forward
Not looking back on what could have been
Yesterday is but a memory to those that hop.

Cold has an earthen tomb

Lost inside of a cave of desolation
Outside I cannot see
Underneath a blanket of worry
Dying every minute the struggle to stay alive
Your handsome smile will be missed but right now things are cloudy.

Creative love in our eyes
Reflection of life in our smile
Young and old please do not cry.

Decayed through the years of torment
Erased like the chalk on a board
Arrest goes the heart
Deep in the wounds of time
Inside the mind is shutdown
Nasty little thing called a life
Sadistic are the people
Instantly judging without giving a care
Dark room of rage
Enclosed from the world being forgotten.

Does
Everything
Alive
Truly
Happen?

Evangeline beauty
Across the seas it is celebrated
Recycle what you no longer need
Treat this world with kindness
Help make it better for the future

Decline your urge to contaminate
Allow for forgiveness and healing
Yearn no longer for today is your day.

Failure is but a means for one to learn
Align your heart and you will see success isn't all it is cracked to be
Internal in the eyes of beholder life is but a knife
Luring you out into the naked the cold to be left alone
Under and over the knife the cuts a path of wonder
Relief from a war torn struggle climb out from beneath the rubble

Even in our darkest moment we should stand proud for we have
achieved something or nothing at all.

Full of
Life
Open to everyone
Wonderful
Exceptional beauty
Reminiscent of love
Swaying in the wind of change.

Life is but a learning experience
It is the wisdom we learn that shape us into the people we are
Forever lost in a moment of endless time
Every heartbeat a story to share.

Would you rather be?

Having a fake smile on your face
Appearing to be like life is good
Passionately feeling sorry for yourself
Personally giving up on what you hold dear
Yesterday's fallen

Or

Having a real smile on your face
Appear to that is life is full of love
Passionately feel proud for yourself
Personally uphold on what you hold dear
Yesterday's risen.

Once lonely
Now I am happy
Entering with pride because I am.

Release this
Aged
Insightful
Nefarious soul.

You can either be

Sadness running through the veins
At the bottom in the world that time has forgotten
Dread and fear run rampant through these parts

Or

Smiling letting the light flow through the veins
A top of the mountain refusing to be the forgotten
Dancing to your favorite tune without a fear to the world

Which would you rather be?

Story
Crowned
As
Reasoning.

Treat
Others
Daily
As
Yourself.

5 FORGOTTEN

My Reality In Vain

Going insane because nothing has gone right for me
failing every challenge that life threw at me
stumbling and falling because my life is a living hell
shot through the heart torn in half
sadness flowing through my veins droplets of sorrow longing to be
let out.

Drowning in a sea of depression tears sucking me in
despair and torment gnawing at my skin
my mind feels light has if my soul flew away
darkness eclipses my heart taking away all the sunshine
confusion slamming me into a wall of doubt.

Why can't anything go right
Why does life have to be filled with fright
Why does happiness slip through my fingers
Why does loneliness seem to be the only thing that lingers
Why does world have to be so cruel?
Answers that will never be known.

My reality is in vain it will never be the same

unless something can take away this pain.

Through The Eyes Of The Forgotten

My gaze is meant to be happiness
Cheer is what I bring
You are all that matters to me
My eyes are open to play
However you pay no attention
I sit and wait for you all day
Your heart is favored in mine
Dancing around with joy being next to you
You tip toed into my soul and I returned the favor
However you pay no attention
What happened today we spent together?
The minutes filled with smiles
The seconds filled with laughter
Why is the box with lights more important than me?
Please explain to me why you no longer pay attention?

Twin or Shadow

Once in a land that time nearly forgotten lived a twin
In the annuals of time his name is written, Ken
Swollen with pain and dripping with sin
Silhouetted against the darkness of his den
Left here pacing wondering why his life begin
Flat hand chopping as if looking like a fin
Lies have been tossed and crossed inside of the bin
Am I a twin or a shadow of my former self?
Bones are broken and words have been spoken that cannot mend
Always messing things up with nothing to commend
Hiding under the bed the message he did send
Lifeless are the breaths that cannot defend
Not even himself can he depend
Wondering what the answer will be once around the bend
I love you being spoken, but this time not as trend
Am I a twin or a shadow of my former self?
Once in a land that time nearly lived a twin
In the annuals of time her name is written, Kin

Swollen with beauty and dripping with sin
Silhouetted against the vibrancy of her den
Left here pacing wondering why her life begin
Flat hand waving as if looking like a fin
Lies have tossed and crossed inside of the bin
Am I a twin or a shadow of my former self?
Bones are strong, and words have spoken helping her to mend
Always everything seemed to go right with lots to commend
Laying on the bed reading the message he did send
Full of life are the breaths that cannot defend
Only to herself can she depend
Whispering the answer that will soon be around the bend
I love you being spoken, but this time it is the trend
Am I a twin or a shadow of my former self?
The message has been sent and received
Now in each other's eyes love they perceive
All left out in the open nothing to deceive
Hearts full of hope neither one naive
Lips joined as one each other's breath they retrieve
Warmth is the embrace that is now conceived
Pain is now gone all but relieved
Are we a twin or a shadow of our former self?

Wayward Soul

Here he goes the wayward soul
Forever on a journey of discovery
Many lessons have been taught, and many more are to be told
Lost in the darkness with only a small light to light the way
Will he ever be discovered, or will he walk alone forever.

Wishful Dream

Wishing for the pain to go away
Inside this nightmare
Serious is the dilemma
Having lost the way

Driving me beyond insanity

Realizing things will never be the same
Encrusted in a tomb of self pity
Alone in this land without sun
May someone have mercy on this soul?

6 FRIENDSHIP

Friends

Friends are like glue they stick to even when you don't want them to
They pick on you for the fun of it or sometimes to be mean
With a smile however their friendship rings true
In our blindest moments they help us to be seen
When we are down and out they are there when we feel blue
Dirtiest secrets to them they will become clean.

Friendship

Troubled
Voiced
Voiceless
Joy
Sorrow
Thankful
Thankless
Sunrise
Boring
Normal
Weird
Rage
Calm
Hugs
Back-stab
Together
Alone
Free
Trapped

7 ENTERTAINMENT

Big Show
Biggest athlete in the world
Intense is your presence

Grabbing a hold with that big hand to choke-slam,

Smiling always in good humor

Have to be one of the best showmen

Open is your heart of gold

Working hard for the fans.

Blaze the Cat

Blazing with fury when you make her mad

Love undeniable for the Sol Emeralds

Almost always shy

Zinging past the obstacles

Eternal protector

Trying to stop Egg-man Nega

Having a heart of fire

Enjoying the company of close of friends

Care taken for her role as princess

Always a step ahead

The fluid movement of dance.

Christian

Captain Charisma is what you call yourself

Having the heart of a lion

Reaction from the crowd always huge

Involved with a nasty dispute with Del Rio

Staying alive even when it seems a loss is at hand

True to yourself you have always stayed

Into the hearts of millions have found yourself

A warrior brave standing tall

Never giving up on the peeps.

Edge

Exceptional ring presence

Dodging the bullets you are good at

Greatness flows through his veins

Enduring the pain you have exceeded all expectations.

Evan Bourne

Engaged are my eyes as you move like Lightning

Victorious most of the time you are not

Against the grain you do shave

Never giving up that chance

Becoming one of the best high fliers

Occasionally getting hurt from your actions

Under and over you do fly like wind

Really exciting to watch your finisher

Not a moment goes by that you don't choose to shine

Even in the darkest moments you shine brighter.

Ghost Adventures

Ghost hunting is our passion

Harboring the voices of the lost

On these nights we are locked in

Strolling through these abandoned buildings

Truths are told from the souls

Adventures spread far and wide

Detours often faced

Vengeance is not our game

Entwined in mystery

Never knowing when to give up

Talking through the digital recorders

Underground we have been

Remembrance for those wish to be heard

Enough is never enough as there is always something to tell

Secrets kept for years

John Cena

Jokester like no other

Having the strength of a few men

On your face is always a smirk of confidence

Never give up never surrender is your motto

Compassion runs through your veins

Encourage others you do

Nation of thousands chant your name

A strong will you possess.

Knuckles

Kaboom goes the rocks as he punches them

Not trusting anyone

Under and over mountains he can climb

Craving the chili dogs

Knuckling past his way through enemies

Lending a hand when it is needed

Enraged defender of the chaos emeralds

Soaring through the air

Thunderous are his punches

Heart of rock

Enormous presence

Egg-man doesn't stand a chance against him

Chaos emeralds are his pride

Having been a former villain

Internal struggle to find himself

Dependent on him are his friends

In his eyes are pain

Never giving up

Always a welcome sight.

Lara Croft

Living legend of adventure

Along the cliffs you do shimmy

Remembrance of treasures past

A tangled web of mystery of and suspense

Crafty you are

Resting in the peace the villains are not

Only guns she trusts

Failure is not option

Today not even death can keep you down.

Legend of Spyro

Legend speaks of a young purple dragon

Ember blasts he creates

Great ice bursts he creates

Earthen power he creates

Nifty elecrtrical rays he creates

Great legacy of a fallen race

Often defeated, but never surrendering

Forests speak of the tales of battle

Sparks is his best friend

Protecting the ones he loves

Yesterday is full of sorrow

Remembering those who he has lost

On the wings of dragon he will rise.

Legend of Zelda

Link has come to stop the Evil Ganondorf

Entangled in a mystery

Granted power by the Triforce of Courage

Enter Death Mountain where the Goron's need your help

Narrow path leads to Zora's river

Deku shrubs abound

On the wings of the wise owl

Fighting for survival

Zelda is the princess we have to save

Enlisting the help of the Ocarina

Legends speak of Shiek

Digging holes to find treasure

Across the fields of Hyrule we travel.

Link

Legendary hero

Internal struggle to survive

No problem he can't solve

Knifing the back of evil.

Miles Tails Prowler

Many challenges he has faced

Inventor of so many things

Living proof of adventure tales

Even in the darkest moments he was always there

Scared of everything but strong enough to prevail

Trusty sidekick of Sonic

Along this tricky paths he does travel

In a flash he begins to fly

Lending a hand to those in need

Silent he usually is

Places he has seen

Rescuing those who need a hand

On the inside he is shy

Will power to make it through

Lighting the way for our boy blue

Encased he has been caught

Robotnik will not win.

Resident Evil

Really scared I was at that opening scene

Evil lurks within these walls

Suspense clawing at the backs of the innocent

Devouring the flesh of misfortune souls

Entombed inside nowhere is safe

Never stand still or your life you forfeit

Truth is but an option that you choose

Enter the realm where sanity has no name

Villain out of your closest comrade

Intestines spread out onto the floor

Life will never be the same again.

Shawn Michael s

Showman of the greatest kind

Having been through everything

Able to climb the ladder of success multiple times

Working hard every day for those you love

Never giving up even when you should have

Making a name for yourself to greatest of extremes

Incredible is your in ring ability

Charisma unmatched

Heart is an understatement for the size you have

A legend you have become

Each day your brought it

Living the boyhood dream

Surely will be missed but never forgotten

Sonic

Speed demon like no other

Onward you always press on

Never giving up on your friends

Into the unknown you travel

Courses of swirls you tackle

Turning into a spin ball of destruction

Head full of spikes

Echindena now an ally

Hallways full of traps

Encircle is the obstacles

Depending on your trusty friend Tails

Greatness you have achieved

Eternal is the night that this is over

Helping save all those who were captured

Over the years a love has blossomed

Granting hope to all you come in contact with.

Stone Cold

Stunning your opponents

Tougher then nails

Only man that can take on the boss

Never letting a beer go unopened

Entering with the sound of shattering glass

Cold as ice

Opening up the cans of whoop ass

Legend of the ring

Don't give a damn about anybody

Steve is his name

Thez press he delivers

Encompassing presence

Victory doesn't matter only kicking ass

Entertainment you deliver

Austin 3:16

Undermining management

Strikes with the venom of a rattlesnake

Thrusting with chair shots

In trust of no one

Never knowing when to give in.

Super Mario Bros.

Spring jump the baddies

Underneath the ground the pipes do lead

Power blocks a plenty

Earning star power

Resourceful is King Koopa

Mischief he does create

A red plumber named Mario always thwarts his plans

Reaching out for the help of his brother Luigi

Inside the castle Princess Peach is captured

Onward always to rescue her

Brother til the end

Restoring the Kingdom to its glory

On this day we celebrate

Stories are told of their legacy.

Thank You Edge

The ladder of greatness has been scaled

Championships accolades throughout the years

Injury paid the toll on the body

Smiles rose from my face watching the matches

Excitement filled the air sometime to intense to watch

Glory is the meaning shown on the tron

Speechless I am left to legacy I grew up watching

One of the best to ever step into the ring

Boots laced up for the best entertainment to offer

Cheering or jeering you always made the impact

I hope your future continues to shine just has bright as your career

In the hall of fame you are bound to be

Thank you for all the memories you have given

Hope to see you again sometime in the horizon.

The Miz

The test time you have withered

Having a mouth bigger then Texas

Even when those who said you fail you succeed

Mic is your tool to get ahead

In the ring you weasel your way out of a fight

Zen is anything, but what you are.

The Killing Joke

All the freaks roam the city tonight

This is for my Father and my Mother too

When you stare you see the gleam in my eyes

Remember that when I am swooping from the skies

Don't want to be delivered so I turn away from the light

Want to make things my own way don't you know

Vengeance fills the inside of this empty shell

With vengeance comes many walks through Hell

Doesn't matter what I do left always becomes right

Endless struggle countless battles every broken bone

Pain is my brother married to torture father to justice

Those worth saving don't even know if they can trust me

Thanks to a failed system the guilty roam free tonight

No matter how many times I put them away they never stay

This hell has become my home sworn to protect

When vengeance comes to hunt you will never detect

To the innocent I have become the guiding light

What doesn't kill me makes stronger

Everything you have been told hold remembrance

Eventually I will make my own deliverance

Still I fell victim to the killing joke.

TMNT

Teenagers at heart no matter the age

Excitement flows from your every battle

Enraged is Ralph most of the time

Ninja skills you have learned throughout the years

Adrenaline flows through Leo's veins

Greatness you are destined for

Entangled in a web of secrets is the Shredder

Mutants are what you are called

Underestimate nothing on your journey

Trust in your brothers and in your master Splinter

Allow for hearts to be open to beauty of this world

Never giving up even in the toughest of spots

Tales are spoken of the silent ones

Never surrendering even when it seems the only option

In the sewers is your home

Newest inventions that Donny has come up with

Jokes Mikey does tell

April was their first friend

Tackling the obstacles is Casey

Understanding the value of life

Recovering from serious injury

Today you bask in the glory of victory

Lessons have been taught that should not be forgotten

Enlightenment brought to your eyes

Stealth is the key always.

8 2012 AND ONWARD

Bullying Must Stop

Beautiful hearts sexist in us all

Untie the knots of hate

Let your eyes see what can not be seen

Lend hands instead of fists

Yearning for freedom from self absorption

In shock and awe we stare to no avail

Never take action we just talk

Grief rings out louder than gunshots.

Mistakes exist in us all please accept

Understand no one is perfect

Surrender to passion and see the shimmering love

Today is lovely for us all.

Share your stories to the world

Towards the sun we must aim

Open your arms to what there is to offer

Please heed this message how would you feel if it was you?

Edge of Souls

People haunt my every move

Pain searing like a stove

Shackled by the feet the spikes did drove

Eyes closed afraid to wake

A brilliant heart they did take

Washed ashore of this diluted lake

In this endless second the sands tick a tomb

Love torn asunder blown like a bomb

Bodies run over the harvesters did comb

A wasteland on the ground that no one wished to placate

Tears shed falling like acid filled flakes

Souls inside the oven continue to bake.

Magnetic Pulse

Beauty has been spotted

Seconds seems like minutes for the time allotted

Gripping my chest feeling like its clotted

Magnetic pulse beats this dying heart

The wind blows her blonde hair lifting the locks of curls

My head begins to spin thoughts lost in a twirl

Eyes now only for her feels like the only girl

Magnetic pulse beats this dying heart

Do I have the courage to hi

Fearing her reply will be simply bye

Nothing left to lose so might go for it shoestrings I tie

Magnetic pulse beats this dying heart

Seeing the blue in her eyes I begin to melt

The red of her shirt brings feelings I never felt

Time to the play the cards that were never dealt

Magnetic pulse beats this dying heart

Hello it begins so simple

Blushing as the cheeks dimple

Feeling like I just climbed a temple

Magnetic pulse beats this dying heart

What can I do for you was her simply reply

My soul lifted to the sky

The look in her eyes they can't deny

I think your really pretty out of my mouth did stutter

Gasping she said nothing not even a mutter

My emotions began to clutter

Magnetic pulse beats this dying heart

I think your really nice, but I prefer to single

Oh I didn't mean by it trying to mingle

Inside my head ashamed did jingle

Magnetic pulse beats this dying heart

Can we at least be friends my simple reply

I am sorry we can't be inside I began to cry

Guess I should be going hitting myself on the thigh

Magnetic pulse beats this dying heart

Guess she had magnetic pulse too or maybe I was distracted

Whatever the cause we were destined to be retracted

For now on I guess I should be careful the way I acted

Magnetic pulse beats this dying heart.

Roscoe

The miles ridden in the grass spanning our hearts through time

Wind flowing freely around us two souls lost in an endless bliss

The seconds seem like years with the drop of a dime

Never could have imagined a moment to happen quite like this

The panels were switched before the puzzle was completed

The picture was left to always remain a blur

My fingers now run through shallow breaths feeling defeated

The trembling of tears with feet that don't want to stir

The image of what could have been if the panels were never switched

My shining star in the sky taken while still shining bright

Your light now shines down upon me afar touching me without twitching

Alone I sit now in the grass thinking about what is right

The wind now blows with your breathe telling me it will be okay

Two souls converge into one and the battle I feel like I have won

Someday soon we will meet again our eyes will meet where they will stay

Life is too short to dwell on what should have been and done

My Roscoe please do not be sad one day we will ride across the galaxy.

Sirene of Serenity

Endless is the grace put out on display

Confident is the picture painted to the world

The screaming in her heart for the fantasy that is to become

Shining star that lights up the corridors of hope

The struggles turn into triumphant joy

A leader of the pack that runs wild with creativity

Words spoken with wisdom always ready to share

Fashion is the glue that holds everything together

Pride rises from the shallows of doubt

Encouragement is the key that unlocks the world

And she is the Sirene of Serenity.

Whispers in the Wild

She said to me you lie to me, and I reply what have I done?
She said we will never be one part.
Thrust like a dart her hand ripped out my heart, she tasted it ever so tart.
I ran out the door to face life's final chore.
Hit faster than a speeding car my flesh tears apart into every scar.
The devil was thrown out of me.
What the hell have I done I decree, but is scream even worth a plea!
Washed along the shore my body begins to quake, and it was my life to take.
Surrounded by the Fey I take their hand to explore without even a delay.
There is no sense here laying in decay, sleep, hope, pray for the end.
What the hell happened to me lost all alone in the land of the free yeah, yeah,
yeah.
The Chief said without a heart you are one of us, and calm now no need to fuss.
I ran into the wild, because a child of the wild is what I have become.
I will hunt her down take her heart just like she took mine.
It will taste ever so sweet, because I will not bow down to defeat again yeah
never again.

The wind speaks ever so silently traveling across the miles to every tree. Scars,
Scars, Scars.
Together now we are whispers in the wild, and we are now deaths child...

One More Reason To Live

The years spent thinking is things good or bad

Trapped between the spaces of sorrow or glad

Mixed into the emotions adding just a tad

Hollow is the life brought before the innocent lad

My Hell became a lot like Heaven from melodies played through the heart

Defeat was the stage of abuse that could never overcome

Shallow in the corner surrounded by the total of the sum

Blisters are the memories of a soul murdered by society alum

Endless are the words that only reach a vast expanse of time succumb

My Hell became a lot like Heaven from the Favorite Color that displayed
affections sweet or tart

A day to be Alone was the moral of Everyday Life that I have lived tight

Today was yesterday's failure but now the future is looking bright

In a sea of darkness of trials your tribulations became my light

If You Want Me oh how those words lifted into such a flight

My Hell became a lot like Heaven with the lyrics that revived a heart

Bitter was the end clogged with so much sin

Can't even remember when this life started to begin

Remembrance was the key to unlock the secret of the kin

Stories of the past are now stories of the old told with skin

My Hell became a lot like Heaven when sorrow of the night became the light of day apart

With the music my spirit was lifted into the sky

Everything coming together for something I could not deny

With the realization that everything was a lie

Rebuilding the boards that were pried

My Hell became a lot like Heaven that started with One Less Reason to every excuse that was once told with a forgotten heart.

Hanging on a Lifetime

Intense fighting spanned the screen

Tears of joy and of sorrow are set out display

Excitement races through my eyes

Lips are shut to intense to say a word

Lessons are taught, and some are loss

People are played, cheated, or unforgiving

Lives are forfeited, and are born

I am hanging on the edge of my seat again

Birds fly into cover

The clouds are darkened with disarray

Rain is sporadic not knowing what to do

Lightning strikes without the sound of thunder

Voices are silenced as the sirens blare

People scurry into cover

Worry caresses the faces

I am hanging on the edge of my seat again

My ears filled with emotions singing so loud

Drums pounding in my chest from the beat

The pulse of energy shot through me

Mosh pit of fans so wild

Lights so brilliant creating a blinding sensation

Shouting for the band can be heard

I am hanging on the edge of my seat again

Cries can be heard from the mother

Pain is felt throughout

Breaths so heavy weighing me down

The doctor exclaims

Cries can be heard from the baby

I am hanging on the edge of my seat again

Tomorrow is the thrill of a new day

The sun shines so brightly on my life

So many things I have accomplished

So many more memories to make

I am hanging on the edge of my seat again

Grown old but grown loved

Not sure how many more battles we can take

Excitement still runs through these eyes

I am hanging on the edge of my seat again

Rollercoaster roaring about from my retirement party

So many lives I have blessed

I am hanging on the edge of my seat again

She dies

I am hanging on the edge of my seat again

We Are Majestic

Sitting at the top of a throne of bones

Skipping down the hall are skulls like stones

The smile that drips with sin from the skin within

The crown of glory with metal wearing thin

Surrounded by a mot of crimson slivers while the dagger is dung into the liver

A Pincess is calling the King is dead stand and deliver

Ravaged hearts abuzz with the flames of yesterdays fears how he waited through the years

A Pincess cries with frozen tears

The Dark Prince stands gallantly in front of the throne of bones

His sword dropping to the floor of stones

To his men he stares braving smiling with victory from within as he wipes the blood from his skin

A Princess shouts with words that are hallowed and thin

The Dark Prince reaches for her hand as he feels the warm shivers as she reaches for her quiver

A Princess shoots with a powerful blow like a raging river

A Dark Prince falls with a gaping wound that no one could hear he intentions left unclear

A Princess rallies the royal army to defeat their foes for she is now a leader of a Kingdom that is left with her command to steer.

ABOUT THE AUTHOR

This book features poems written by Robert Hicks from a young age up to present day. His influences for the poetry comes from his favorite bands, movies, video games, and books. He currently lives in Heath, Ohio where the woods around also serve as inspiration.